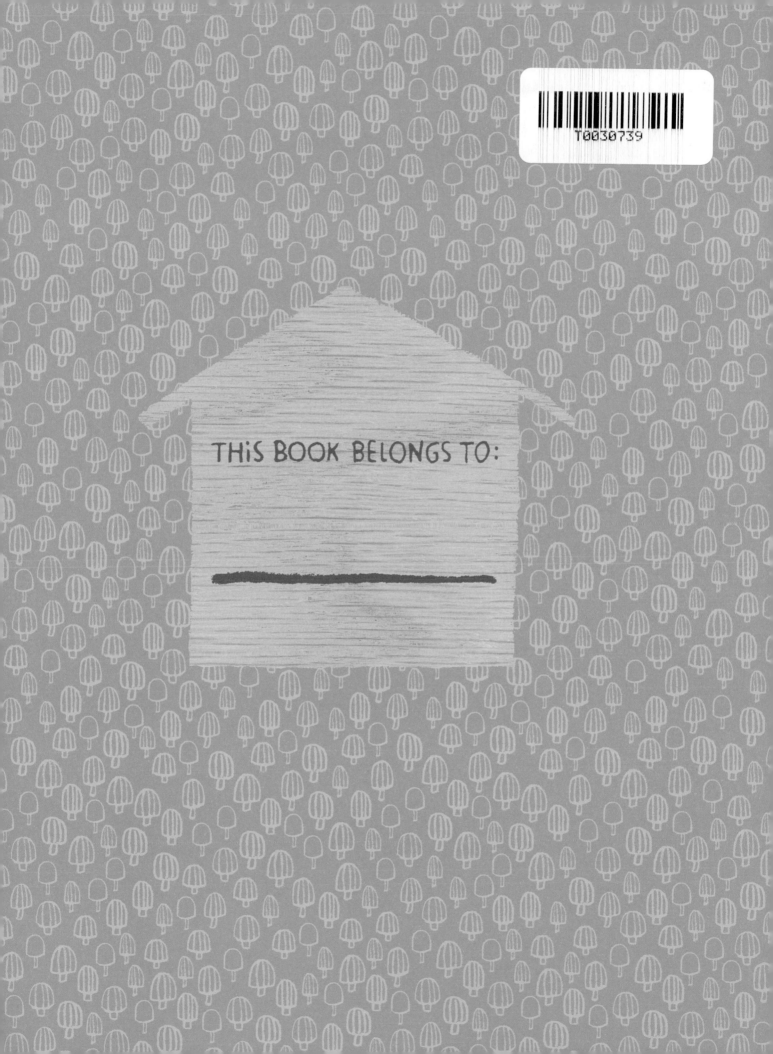

THIS BOOK BELONGS TO:

_____

To my brother, Bryan,
whose childhood love of nature and habitats
inspired me at an early age to be fascinated
with the natural world

BEACH LANE BOOKS
An imprint of Simon & Schuster Children's Publishing Division
1230 Avenue of the Americas, New York, New York 10020 • © 2024 by Amy Hevron • Book design by Lauren Rille © 2024 by Simon & Schuster, Inc. • All rights reserved, including the right of reproduction in whole or in part in any form. • BEACH LANE BOOKS and colophon are trademarks of Simon & Schuster, Inc. • Simon & Schuster: Celebrating 100 Years of Publishing in 2024 • For information about special discounts for bulk purchases, please contact Simon & Schuster Special Sales at 1-866-506-1949 or business@simonandschuster.com. • The Simon & Schuster Speakers Bureau can bring authors to your live event. For more information or to book an event, contact the Simon & Schuster Speakers Bureau at 1-866-248-3049 or visit our website at www.simonspeakers.com. • The text for this book was set in Fairplex. • The illustrations for this book were rendered in acrylic, marker, and pencil on Bristol board and digitally collaged. • Manufactured in China • 1023 SCP • First Edition • 10 9 8 7 6 5 4 3 2 1 • Library of Congress Cataloging-in-Publication Data • Names: Hevron, Amy, author. • Title: Log life / Amy Hevron. • Description: First edition. | New York : Beach Lane Books, 2024. | Series: Tiny habitats | Includes bibliographical references. | Audience: Ages 4—8 | Audience: Grades 2—3 | Summary: "A nonfiction picture book about the tiny world of nurse log habitats."— Provided by publisher. • Identifiers: LCCN 2023005831 (print) | LCCN 2023005832 (ebook) | ISBN 9781665934985 (hardcover) | ISBN 9781665934992 (ebook) • Subjects: LCSH: Forest ecology—Juvenile literature. | Forest animals—Habitations—Juvenile literature. | Forest litter—Juvenile literature. • Classification: LCC QH541.5.F6 H475 2024 (print) | LCC QH541.5.F6 (ebook) | DDC 577.3—dc23/eng/20230614 • LC record available at https://lccn.loc.gov/2023005831 • LC ebook record available at https://lccn.loc.gov/2023005832

A TiNY HABiTATS BOOK

log
life

Amy Hevron

Beach Lane Books • New York London Toronto Sydney New Delhi

Once there stood a giant
fir tree that stretched to the sun.

One stormy day, a great gust came.

The tree creaked

and cracked

and **COLLAPSED!**

When the storm passed,
the sun shined down through
an opening in the canopy.

And the tree's new life
as a nurse log began.

spring

year 1

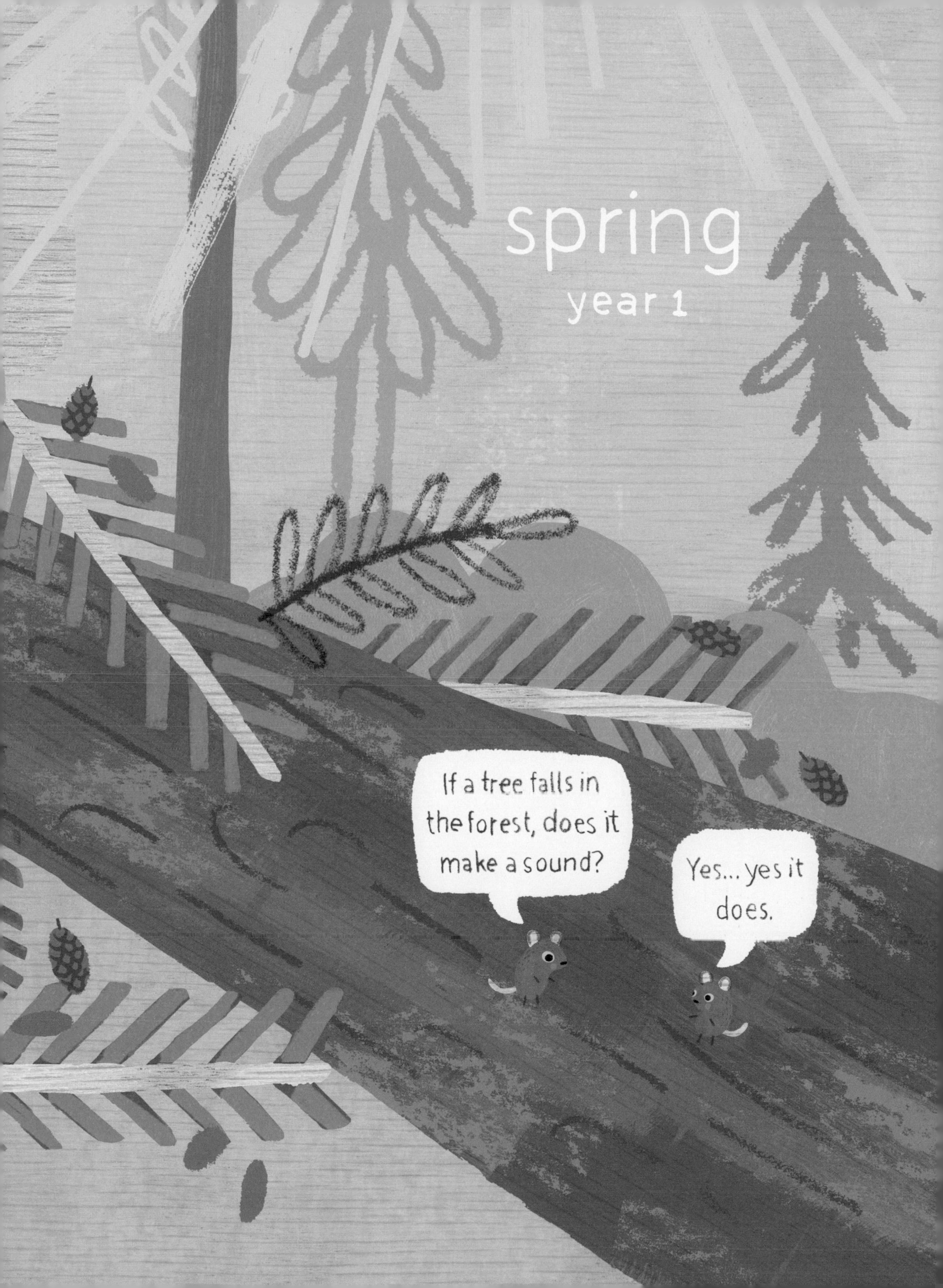

Fungi were the first to arrive.
They feasted on the damp wood.

They invited their
lichen friends,

who invited their
liverwort friends,

who invited their
hornwort friends,

who invited their
chicken mushroom friends.

It was a big,
mushroomy party!

Hooray!

Soon, beetles moved in.

And carpenter ants arrived.

Which brought nuthatches and warblers and—

KNOCK,
KNOCK!

A woodpecker!

One day, a squirrel bounded in.

Bark! Bark! Bark!

He chowed down on fir cones.
Seeds scattered everywhere . . .

and some found homes in cracks and crannies.

Plop!

Before long, a new fir tree
sprouted and stretched
to the sun.

On dry days, the nurse log was a soggy shelter to all kinds of critters.

summer
year 10

Snails vacayed in the decay.

Voles nibbled on seeds in the shade.

Salamanders slithered into the hollows.

Tree frogs cooled down in the dark dens.

Meanwhile, the young fir tree
clung on and waited for rain.

On rainy days, the nurse log became
a beautiful tapestry of . . .

fancy fern fronds,

autumn
year 100

munching banana slugs,

and shimmering slime molds.

Sometimes big critters would visit.

Sometimes the nurse log helped the little critters hide away.

Meanwhile, the fir tree grew tall with roots
that stretched over the nurse log.

On cold days, everyone
cuddled inside the nurse log.

Squirrels dozed in its dark dens.

Martens slept in its mossy hollows.

A cougar snoozed in its cozy crevices.

Nuthatches nested in its warm nooks.

Meanwhile, the fir tree soared above on
stilt-like roots that now stretched over
the nurse log all the way to the forest floor.

Over time, the nurse log's soggy shelters
and mossy hollows have disappeared.

spring
year 1000

In its place now,
the giant fir tree stands
and stretches to the sun.

Until one stormy day, a great gust will catch the giant fir.

It will creak

and crack

and COLLAPSE!

And nurse-log life will begin once again.

northern
spotted owl

Roosevelt elk

red-breasted
nuthatch

Wilson's
warbler

red-backed voles

banana slug

Pacific tree
frogs

torrent
salamander

Hey, everybody!
flying squirrel
pileated woodpecker
silver-spotted tiger moths
red-blue checkered beetle
pine marten
Douglas squirrel
millipede

More about Nurse-Log Habitats

Nurse logs are tiny ecosystems that are home to hundreds of rare and important life-forms. This story showcases a nurse-log habitat in an old-growth, temperate rain forest in the Pacific Northwest of the United States. Many of the oldest evergreens on the planet are found in this part of the world. One such evergreen, the Douglas fir, can live up to a thousand years. When these old giants fall to the forest floor, they can take centuries to decompose. As they slowly break down, they provide nutrients and protection throughout the seasons for hundreds of years.

In spring, nurse logs become elevated gardens, with moist, fertilized soil to help tree seedlings and other plant life grow. In dry summer months, soggy nurse logs retain their moisture and are a water source for plants and provide damp hideaways for various mammals and amphibians. In turn, the mammals and amphibians become food for predators, like the northern spotted owl. In fall, the raised perch helps seedlings and plant life avoid being buried in autumn debris. And in winter, nurse logs provide dens and shelters for all sorts of critters.

Here are a few old-growth forests in the United States where you can visit nurse-log habitats: Tongass National Forest in Alaska, Ouachita National Forest in Arkansas, Redwood National Park in California, Mohawk Trail State Forest in Massachusetts, Itasca Wilderness Sanctuary in Minnesota, Willamette National Forest in Oregon, and Olympic National Park in Washington.

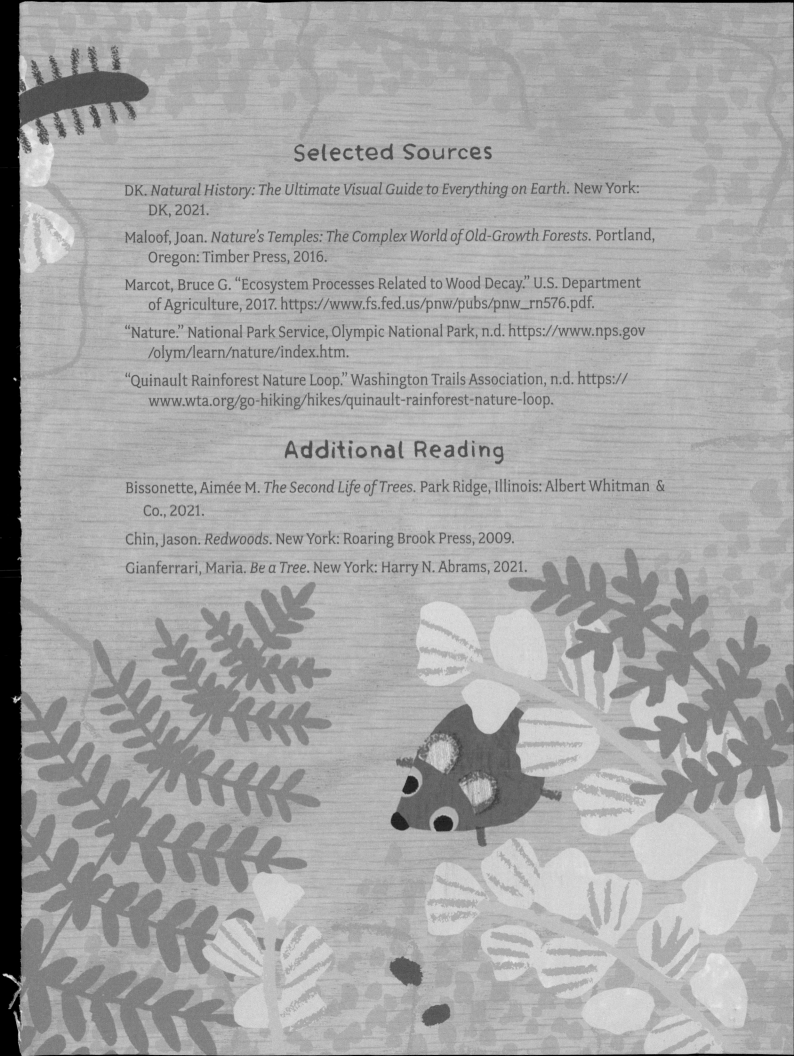

Selected Sources

DK. *Natural History: The Ultimate Visual Guide to Everything on Earth*. New York: DK, 2021.

Maloof, Joan. *Nature's Temples: The Complex World of Old-Growth Forests*. Portland, Oregon: Timber Press, 2016.

Marcot, Bruce G. "Ecosystem Processes Related to Wood Decay." U.S. Department of Agriculture, 2017. https://www.fs.fed.us/pnw/pubs/pnw_rn576.pdf.

"Nature." National Park Service, Olympic National Park, n.d. https://www.nps.gov/olym/learn/nature/index.htm.

"Quinault Rainforest Nature Loop." Washington Trails Association, n.d. https://www.wta.org/go-hiking/hikes/quinault-rainforest-nature-loop.

Additional Reading

Bissonette, Aimée M. *The Second Life of Trees*. Park Ridge, Illinois: Albert Whitman & Co., 2021.

Chin, Jason. *Redwoods*. New York: Roaring Brook Press, 2009.

Gianferrari, Maria. *Be a Tree*. New York: Harry N. Abrams, 2021.